THE AMERICAN REVOLUTION

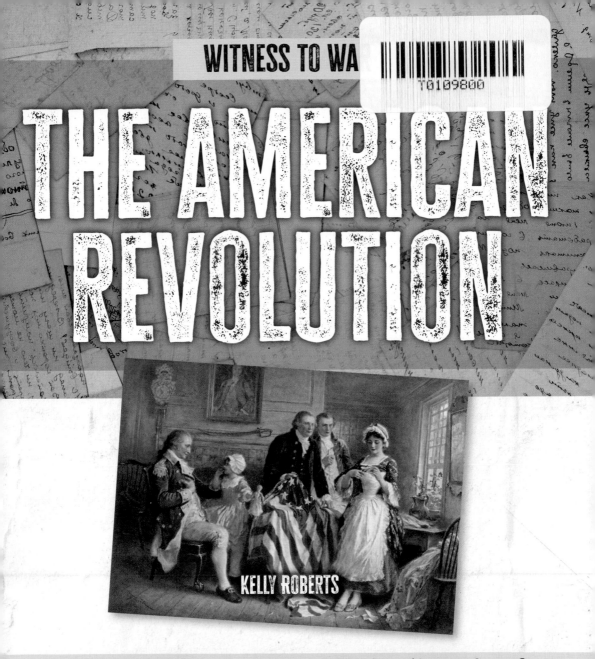

KELLY ROBERTS

What can we learn from the people who witnessed war?

CHERITON
CHILDREN'S BOOKS

Published in 2025 by **Cheriton Children's Books**
1 Bank Drive West, Shrewsbury, Shropshire, SY3 9DJ, UK

Copyright 2025 Cheriton Children's Books

First Edition

Author: Kelly Roberts
Designer: Paul Myerscough
Editor: Sarah Eason
Proofreader: Katie Dicker

Printed in China

Please visit our website,
www.cheritonchildrensbooks.com
to see more of our high-quality books.

CONTENTS

CHAPTER 1

THE AMERICAN REVOLUTION

A revolution is a complete change in a country's government. In the course of history, some revolutions have been peaceful. Many, though, have been fought as bloody wars. The revolution that shaped the United States was one such war.

Affecting a Nation

For the war's duration (1775–1783) and beyond, it would affect the lives of every man, woman, and child who lived through it, as well as generations to come. They would witness the devastation of war—and in doing so, become a witness to history. In this book we will look at some of their stories and their words as witnesses to war.

WITNESSES TO WAR

In this book we will hear the words of witnesses to the war: the people who experienced the conflict firsthand. We'll discover what impact the war had on them and what we can learn from their accounts. In each case, read the source and the notes, then try to answer the questions.

This is one of the most famous images of the American Revolution. It is named *Yankee Doodle* and was created for the 1876 centenary celebrations of American independence from Britain.

Ruled from Afar

Before the American Revolution, the country that we know as the United States did not exist. Instead, there were 13 loosely connected British **colonies** along the Atlantic coast of North America. From 1760, the British colonies were controlled by Great Britain.

Wanting to Break Free

Over time, tensions grew between the colonists—who were mostly British settlers—and the British government. They disagreed over many issues, especially those of **taxes** and money. Many colonists believed that they were being treated unfairly. They decided that their only choice was to declare themselves a new, independent country, free to make its own rules, and revolution inevitably followed.

Creating America

The American Revolution was neither the longest nor the bloodiest war in US history, but it is one of the most important. It created the documents that designed the US government and shaped the country that exists today. In that sense, Americans still live with its effects.

Unimaginable Change

When Christopher Columbus arrived in America in 1492, it would have been impossible to imagine how the continent of North America would change over the next few hundred years. Different European countries, including Spain, Portugal, and France, established colonies in the new land. However, it was England, together with Wales and Scotland, that ultimately had the most success in colonizing what is now the East Coast of the United States.

Settling the New World

The first permanent English settlement in North America was Jamestown, founded in the Colony of Virginia in 1607. A few years later, in 1620, the settlers we know as the Pilgrims arrived on the *Mayflower*. They created the Plymouth Colony, in Massachusetts.

English colonists sailed to America in the hope of creating a new life in a new land.

Three Types

Before the American Revolution, the British had three types of colonies in North America—**royal colonies**, **proprietary colonies**, and **charter colonies**. A royal, or crown, colony was controlled by a governor who was chosen by the king. Just before the revolution, most of the 13 colonies were royal colonies. Proprietary colonies were areas of land given by the king to a person or family—usually to reward loyalty or service. The person, or proprietor, was responsible for governing the colony, but still answered to the king. Pennsylvania, Maryland, and Delaware were all proprietary colonies.

Give and Take

In the third type of colony, the **charter** colony, the king granted a charter to the governing body of the colony. The charter was an official document setting out the rules by which the colony would be run. Connecticut and Rhode Island were both charter colonies. At any time, the king could revoke, or take away, this charter and turn the colony into a royal colony. The Massachusetts Bay Colony, for example, had its charter revoked in 1684.

A Delicate Relationship

The relationship between Great Britain and its North American colonies was very important. However, it was also quite fragile. Britain saw the colonies as a means to make and raise money. That is because early settlers often went to the New World to make their fortunes. But as time went on, many colonists began to see a chance to gain much more than money.

The British colonies of North America were ruled by King George III of Great Britain.

Searching for Wealth and Freedom

The early colonists—mainly men—came to North America thinking more about business ventures than raising families. Other colonists, such as the Pilgrims, came to the New World looking for religious freedom. Many wanted to separate from the Church of England and form their own religious groups. To do so, they believed they would need to take some political control of their colonies.

Success and Hardship

The Pilgrims founded Plymouth Colony, in what is today Massachusetts. Conditions were harsh, but the settlers worked together to create one of the earliest successful British colonies in North America. Families usually included five to six children, though about 12 percent of children died in their first year.

Rich in Resources

Over time, settlers learned to grow food and benefit from North America's **resources**. Though life was difficult, communities began to thrive and expand. Tobacco became an important crop, especially in the southern colonies. Colonists began bringing Africans to North America to work as enslaved people on their plantations. As colonies grew, their relationship with Britain and their forms of government became even more important issues, particularly because of taxes.

Free Beliefs

The Pilgrims hoped for the chance to practice their religious beliefs without persecution.

This illustration shows the early Pilgrims who sought a new life in America. They are shown holding their Bibles.

This illustration shows Native Americans who supported the French attacking British soldiers and civilians in 1757 during the French and Indian War (see below).

Raising Money

The French and Indian War (1754–1763) was part of a worldwide nine-year-long war between Great Britain and France, and was fought over the colonies that each country held in North America. Although Great Britain won the war, the fight had left the country in great debt. As a result, it created new taxes on the colonies and raised existing taxes to help pay the debt. Some Native American peoples supported the French while others supported the British, during the war over land in North America.

The Heavy Cost of Living

The Sugar Act of 1764 placed additional taxes on sugar and other products such as wine, coffee, and a type of dye called indigo. These products were important to colonial families, so the higher prices meant they had less money to spend on other things that their families needed to survive. Meanwhile, those who sold the products worried that because fewer people could afford to buy them, they would go out of business, and that they would not be able to support their families.

CHAPTER 2

TENSIONS GROW

Many in the colonies were not doing well financially during the mid-1700s. People also worried about the future. Some colonists had hoped that the British victory in the French and Indian War would mean more land to settle with their families. However, to protect Native American territory, the British created the Proclamation of 1763, which stopped colonists from settling in new territories, forcing them to remain on the East Coast. Settlers who had already bought land beyond the East Coast boundary were forced to leave it.

PRIMARY SOURCE

The Boston Massacre

In 1770, five colonists were killed by British soldiers during a protest (see page 11). A few weeks later this engraving, titled the Boston Massacre, depicted the event. What effect do you think the title "Boston Massacre" had on the colonists?

Anger and Protest

In 1765, another tax was created when the Stamp Act was passed. It made colonists pay a tax on printed materials, such as newspapers and legal documents. This made the colonists even angrier, and people began to protest the new taxes. In 1766, both the Sugar Act and Stamp Act were **repealed**, or stopped, but many colonists were becoming more and more unhappy with the way that Great Britain was governing them. By 1770, tensions between colonists and British soldiers were at an all-time high, and on March 5, a small group of British soldiers fired into an angry crowd of colonists. They killed five men.

Paul Revere was a talented engraver who lived in Boston. His engraving (page 10) is another famous image of the war.

WITNESS TO WAR

Captain Thomas Preston was part of the group of British soldiers who opened fire on the colonists in 1770. He says his soldiers fired without orders. This is part of his account:

"On my asking the soldiers why they fired without orders, they said they heard the word fire and supposed it came from me. This might be the case as many of the mob called out fire, fire, but I assured the men that I gave no such order; that my words were, don't fire, stop your firing. In short, it was scarcely possible for the soldiers to know who said fire, or don't fire, or stop your firing."

Do you think that, in the chaos of the conflict, the British soldiers may have thought they heard the command to fire?

Do you think the colonists may have been calling out "fire," and if so, why?

No Representation

Under the current form of US government, elections are held in which people can vote on who will represent them in local, state, and federal government. Each state sends two representatives to the Senate and a proportionate number to the House of Representatives. Together, these two bodies make up the US Congress, which makes laws. Today, we often take it for granted that we have a say in how the government is run. However, this was not the case for colonists before the American Revolution.

To Tax or Not to Tax?

Though the British repealed the Sugar Act and the Stamp Act, they still believed they had a right to tax the colonies in any way they chose. They considered taxes to be no different from any other law. Many colonists, on the other hand, began to openly question why they should be taxed by the British **Parliament** when they were not represented in that parliament.

PRIMARY SOURCE

Sons of Liberty

Growing numbers of people joined forces to protest British control, and began to actively encourage others to do so. This advertisement was created by a group called the **Sons of Liberty**, which encouraged active rebellion against the British Government and its taxation of the colonies. What do you think they meant by asking "friends to the Liberties, and Trade of America" to attend the advertized meeting?

ADVERTISEMENT.

THE Members of the Affociation of the Sons of Liberty, are requefted to meet at the City-Hall, at one o'Clock, To-morrow, (being Friday) on Bufinefs of the utmoft Importance ;—And every other Friend to the Liberties, and Trade of America, are hereby moft cordially invited, to meet at the fame Time and Place. *The Committee of the Affociation.*

Thurfday, NEW-YORK, 16th December, 1773.

No Vote, No Tax!

The idea of rebellion grew stronger with the passage of the Townshend Acts (1767–1768), which included taxes on glass and paper. Colonists argued that, because they did not have a right to vote and send a representative to Parliament, the Parliament had no right to impose taxes on them.

Tea Is the Trigger

In 1773, the British passed the Tea Act. To help the British East India Company, which had a huge amount of tea stored in England, the act lowered the cost of tea sold to the colonies. This undercut local prices, and many colonists saw it as a way of forcing them to buy from the British company.

On the night of December 16, 1773, the Sons of Liberty dressed up as Native Americans. They then snuck aboard three East India Company ships in Boston Harbor, and dumped 342 crates of their tea into the water, destroying it. This rebellious act became known as the Boston Tea Party.

WITNESS TO WAR

George Hewes was a shoemaker who took part in the Boston Tea Party. This is part of his account:

Why do you think the British soldiers did not make any attempt to arrest the colonists? What may have stopped them?

"I immediately dressed myself in the costume of an Indian, equipped with a small hatchet ... We then were ordered by our commander to open the hatches and take out all the chests of tea and throw them overboard ... We were surrounded by British armed ships, but no attempt was made to resist us."

We Will Rule!

To punish the people of Massachusetts for the Boston Tea Party, the British Parliament passed a group of five laws in 1774. The British called these laws the Coercive Acts; the colonists named them the Intolerable Acts. The first allowed the governor of a colony, who was appointed by the king, to move the trial of a royal official to another colony or even back to England if he believed a colonial jury would not be fair. Another act required nearly all appointments to governing positions in the Massachusetts Bay Colony to be made by the governor, the king, or parliament. It also limited the number of town meetings Massachusetts colonists could hold.

The colonists who took part in the Boston Tea Party disguised themselves as Mohawk Native Americans. The colonists used the Mohawk as a symbol of America during the Revolution.

Insults and Anger

A third act allowed British troops to stay in the homes of colonists and other buildings. A fourth act closed Boston Harbor until the British East India Company had been repaid for the tea destroyed during the Boston Tea Party. A fifth act was favorable to Quebec, offering its French residents civil government and religious freedom. Although this last act was not directly related to the American colonies, many colonists considered it an insult.

Deciding How to Act

The Intolerable Acts were meant to stop the rebellious colonists, but the colonists thought the Acts were cruel and severe. They just made people even angrier. Public outcry at the harsh Acts grew and the colonists gathered to discuss how they should respond to the continuing unfairness of the British. They decided to work together to resolve their common dispute. They formed the First Continental Congress to figure out what they should do.

PRIMARY SOURCE

Not a Happy Tea Party

This cartoon was created after the Boston Tea Party. It shows tea being poured down a person's throat. The people pouring the tea represent the British. What figure do you think represents the colonists, and why?

Boston cannonaded.

Boston Port Bill.

CHAPTER 3

THE ROAD TO WAR

To respond to the Intolerable Acts, the First Continental Congress was called. It was a meeting of representatives from 12 of the 13 colonies. The aim of the meeting was to find a way to show the unity of the colonies to Great Britain, and to help resolve the problems between them. The First Continental Congress met from September 5 to October 26, 1774. It was attended by 56 **delegates** from 12 colonies. However, not all of the colonies had the same ideas about how to handle the British.

The First Continental Congress meeting took place in Carpenters' Hall, in Philadelphia, Pennsylvania.

THE FIRST CONTINENTAL CONGRESS · 1774

Different Viewpoints

Some colonists wanted to convince Great Britain to repeal the Intolerable Acts and find a peaceful solution to the conflict. Some wanted to remain British colonies, but find a way to be represented in Parliament. Others wanted to cut ties with the British and become independent.

Home-Grown Army

The First Continental Congress had arranged for a further meeting to take place in May of 1775. But, meanwhile, a rebel group in Massachusetts had begun to train a **militia**—a group of volunteer or citizen soldiers. Members of a militia were generally not well-trained fighters. They did not have uniforms and usually had to provide their own weapons.

Battles and Beginnings

Great Britain now considered Massachusetts to be in a state of rebellion. In April 1775, British troops were sent to destroy supplies being held by the militia in the town of Concord. On April 19, in Lexington, the British met the small local militia, who had been warned they were coming. Neither side expected a battle, but a gunshot went off, and the British began to fire at the militia.

WITNESS TO WAR

Winthrop Sargent was a colonial soldier who fought at the Battle of Lexington. This is part of his account:

"It was very bloody for seven hours. It's conjectured that one half the soldiers at least are killed ... When I reflect and consider that the fight was between those whose parents but a few generations ago were brothers, I shudder at the thought, and there's no knowing where our calamities will end."

What effect do you think the death of at least half of the soldiers may have had on the remaining soldiers?

What do you think Winthrop means by "there's no knowing where our calamities will end"?

Calamities means problems and distress.

Second Congress, Same Challenges

By the time the Second Continental Congress was due to meet, a lot had happened. The British and the colonists, often known as the **Patriots**, were at war. Although the goals of the Second Continental Congress would be different from those of the first, it would face many of the same problems.

Fight or Friendship?

Many of the delegates from the First Continental Congress, such as John Adams and Roger Sherman, attended the Second Continental Congress, too. Benjamin Franklin, John Hancock, and Thomas Jefferson were also there.

While many of the delegates still wanted to settle matters peacefully with the British and remain British colonies, a growing number believed independence was the only answer to their issues with Britain.

George Washington to Lead

The Second Continental Congress, which began meeting on May 10, 1775, in Philadelphia, quickly took charge of the war effort. On June 14, the Continental army was created and George Washington was made its commanding general. He had been a senior officer during the French and Indian War and had seen firsthand the tactics, strengths, and weaknesses of the British army. This knowledge would be very valuable to the Patriots.

George Washington came from a wealthy family of tobacco farmers.

Residence of the Washington Family *

George Washington grew up on a tobacco plantation in Virginia, where his British ancestors had settled in 1657.

Holding Out an Olive Branch

The Olive Branch Petition was written by Congress members led by John Dickinson, who wanted to emphasize their loyalty and make peace with Britain. It was sent to England in July 1775. The words of the Petition are shown below:

"Could we represent in their full force the sentiments that agitate the minds of us your dutiful subjects, we are persuaded your Majesty would ascribe any seeming deviation from reverence in our language, and even in our conduct, not to any reprehensible intention, but to the impossibility of reconciling the usual appearances of respect with a just attention to our own preservation against those artful and cruel enemies who abuse your royal confidence and authority, for the purpose of effecting our destruction."

However, at the same time that the Petition was sent to the king, another letter was discovered by the British. It was from John Adams, and talked about going to war. The letter was sent to England and shown to the king. As a result, King George declared the colonies in rebellion.

We Will Be Independent!

By the summer of 1776, the American Revolution had been underway for more than a year. The fighting was fierce and hard, and the Continental Congress knew that they might need help to continue their effort against the British. However, they knew that no European country would make an **alliance** with the colonies while they were still under British control. There was only one option left to them: they needed to declare themselves an independent country.

Writing and Publishing

Jefferson wrote a first **draft**, then brought it to the others to discuss and make changes. The **committee** wrote another draft, then presented it to the rest of the delegates on June 28. After more editing, the Congress voted to pass the Declaration of Independence on July 2. On July 4, the day now celebrated as Independence Day, the Declaration was finally adopted and printed for the general public.

Delegates for Independence

On August 2, the Declaration of Independence was signed by 56 delegates. A few of the delegates, such as John Dickinson, refused to sign the document. Others signed, even though they had voted against its passage. Though they might not have agreed with the creation of a new independent country, they wanted to show a united front.

Five Key Players

To create the declaration, the Congress appointed a group called the Committee of Five on June 11, 1776. The committee included Thomas Jefferson, John Adams, Roger Sherman, Robert R. Livingston, and Benjamin Franklin.

The Committee of Five decided that Thomas Jefferson (right) should write a draft of the declaration.

WITNESS TO WAR

In 1822, John Adams wrote about the drawing up of the declaration. This is an extract:

"... There were other expressions which I would not have inserted if I had drawn it up, particularly that which called the King tyrant I thought this too personal, for I never believed George to be a tyrant in disposition and in nature; I always believed him to be deceived by his courtiers on both sides of the Atlantic ..."

A tyrant is a person who rules cruelly.

Who do you believe John Adams thought was responsible for the hardship imposed on colonists by the British?

Courtiers are advisors to a king or queen.

This painting shows the Declaration of Independence being presented to the Continental Congress.

The Battleground

The American Revolution lasted nearly eight years, from the first shot to the last. Over that time, there were many important battles between the Continental army and the British army.

Casualties of War

Some battles are considered important because of the high number of **casualties**. Others are remembered because they turned the tide of the war in one direction or the other. For the families who lived through the American Revolution, though, each casualty was devastating. These battles were not fought by professional soldiers, but by ordinary colonists. The loss of a husband, father, son, or brother cost families dearly.

Turning a Corner

While the Battles of Lexington and Concord marked the start of the war, the next major turning point was the capture of Fort Ticonderoga in New York State, in May 1775. A small militia called the Green Mountain Boys raided Fort Ticonderoga and two other forts, capturing cannons and other military supplies. The **artillery** taken was brought to Massachusetts and used to force the British to withdraw from Boston.

On their third advance at the Battle of Bunker Hill (see page 23), the British were able to take the hill, but many were killed, and more than 800 were wounded.

Heavy Losses

The bloodiest battle of the war would occur just a month later. On June 17, 1775, colonial and British troops met at the Battle of Bunker Hill, near Boston. The British troops advanced on the colonial soldiers, who were holding Breed's Hill. During two assaults, the colonial forces fired on the lines of British soldiers, killing several officers and wounding hundreds.

The Battle of Trenton, which took place on December 26, 1776, was another important turning point during the war.

The Fight for Long Island

Another battle known both as the Battle of Long Island and the Battle of Brooklyn took place on August 27, 1776. It involved more troops than any other battle of the war.

PRIMARY SOURCE

A Call to Arms

This poster was used to try and recruit men to the Continental army. What impact do you think the poster may have had on colonial men? What do you think the words "against the hostile designs of foreign enemies" mean?

THE UNITED STATES,
Against the hostile defign of foreign enemies,

TO ALL BRAVE, HEALTHY, ABLE BODIED, AND WELL
DISPOSED YOUNG MEN,
IN THIS NEIGHBOURHOOD, WHO HAVE ANY INCLINATION TO JOIN THE TROOPS,
NOW RAISING UNDER
GENERAL WASHINGTON,
FOR THE DEFENCE OF THE
LIBERTIES AND INDEPENDENCE
OF THE UNITED STATES,
Against the hostile defign of foreign enemies,

TAKE NOTICE,

CHAPTER 4

WOMEN AND THE WAR

Before the revolution, most colonists lived in rural areas outside of cities or large towns. Many either owned or worked on farms. While men were responsible for much of the farm labor, women took care of the household duties. They sewed, cleaned, washed clothes, and prepared food. Other tasks included gardening, milking cows, and preserving meats. Things changed dramatically when the war gathered pace.

Boycotting Britain

As the revolution began, a woman's role in the household took on great significance. Although the governing bodies, made up of men, proposed **boycotts** of British goods, it fell to individual households—and especially women—to put these boycotts into action. During the revolution, women across the colonies stopped ordering clothes and fabrics from England. Many were active in the homespun movement, which encouraged women to weave and spin their own cloth instead of purchasing it from England. They also boycotted British tea and other goods. It became a point of pride to buy goods made in the colonies.

The First American Flag

One woman named Betsy Ross is even credited with creating the first American flag. No one knows if this is true, but it is known that Betsy and her husband, John Ross, ran an upholstery store in Philadelphia and made flags as part of their business. When John was killed in the war, Betsy continued to run the business on her own, which was quite remarkable for a woman at the time.

Betsy Ross, shown in this image, is said to have designed and sewn the original American flag.

WITNESS TO WAR

These are the words of Penelope Barker, a woman from North Carolina who organized the Edenton Tea Party, which took place on October 25, 1775. At the event, 51 women signed a document stating that they would boycott British tea and other goods.

"... we women have taken too long to let our voices be heard. We are signing our names to a document, not hiding ourselves behind costumes like the men in Boston did at their tea party. The British will know who we are."

Penelope says she and other women are putting their names to the document, and not hiding from the British in a costume. What risks may the women have been taking by openly challenging the British? Why do you think they were willing to do so?

Women Warriors

The colonial militias, and later the Continental army, were not made up of professional soldiers, but of everyday colonists. Many of these men left their work and families behind when they went off to fight. Wives, mothers, sisters, and daughters had to look after homes, farms, and businesses. Instead of staying at home, however, some women chose to go off to war, too. One of the most famous accounts of female fighters is that of "Molly Pitcher," a wife who is said to have fought alongside her husband. She became a legendary figure of the war.

Fearless Molly at Monmouth

It is not certain where the nickname "Molly Pitcher" came from, but the legend of Molly Pitcher is well known. It may have come from the real story of a camp follower named Mary Ludwig Hays. At the Battle of Monmouth, in June 1778, Mary Hays' husband was injured while firing a cannon. Mary Hays, who had been carrying water to the troops, took her husband's place firing a cannon.

Molly Pitcher is shown in this illustration, still firing the cannon, even after she was almost hit by enemy fire.

WITNESS TO WAR

One young colonial soldier, Joseph Plumb Martin (whose second account you'll read on page 33), remembered Molly Pitcher in his diaries, describing her as:

" *A woman whose husband belonged to the artillery and who was then attached to a piece in the engagement, attended with her husband at the piece the whole time. While in the act of reaching [for] a cartridge ... a cannon shot from the enemy passed directly between her legs without doing any other damage than carrying away all the lower part of her petticoat.*"

How do you think men in the Continental army reacted to Molly? Do you think her actions may have inspired other colonial women?

Into Battle

Deborah Sampson is another famous female soldier who fought in the war. She had been a school teacher before the Revolution, and when war broke out Deborah decided to join the Continental army. She entered the army in 1782, disguised as a man and under the name of Robert Shurtleff. Her true identity was not discovered until 1783, when she had to be treated for fever in an army camp. She was then discharged from the army.

A number of other women chose not to fight but to follow their husbands into battle because they did not feel safe staying in their homes alone.

This was especially true of women who lived in areas occupied by the British. Other women simply wanted to stay near their husbands.

Life in an Army Camp

Women who accompanied men into army camps were called camp followers. They did not fight in battles, but they supported the men who did by cooking, washing and sewing clothes, and even acting as nurses. They helped with the everyday chores that allowed the camps to run smoothly. Some think there might have been as many as 20,000 women in army camps during the war.

A Giant Divide

Before the time of the American Revolution, colonists considered themselves British, although they lived thousands of miles from England. For many, that loyalty to England did not end when the fighting began. The division between those who believed in independence and those who supported the British split families and turned neighbors and friends against each other.

Two Sides, Two Names

Colonists who believed in independence were called Patriots, while those who stayed loyal to England were called **Loyalists**. It is thought that about 20 percent of colonists remained loyal to England. Choosing whether to be a Patriot or a Loyalist was an important decision that could change your life forever. When Charleston in South Carolina fell to the British in 1780, the women in charge of households had to choose to swear loyalty to Britain or be banished. Two women, Mary Noles and Elizabeth Owen, refused to swear. They were banished from the city along with more than 120 other Patriot women and children.

PRIMARY SOURCE

Sending a Message

This portrait of Elizabeth Theus, a young woman during the time of the American Revolution, shows her wearing a militia outfit and a musket and powder horn crown on her head. What message do you think the artist intended to show with the use of such imagery?

Families at War

Back then—as now—family members did not always agree with each other on political matters. Families were often torn apart, with some members calling themselves Loyalists and others Patriots. It could be very difficult for women who disagreed with their husbands' positions. Women generally did not have a voice in politics. If a man was a Loyalist, it was assumed that his wife was as well, and then the entire family could be targeted.

War and Divorce

During the Revolution, many women who strongly supported one side or the other began taking a public stance, even if it meant going against their husbands or other family members. While divorce had been very rare up to that time, the government began to allow Patriot women to divorce their Loyalist husbands.

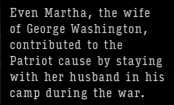

Even Martha, the wife of George Washington, contributed to the Patriot cause by staying with her husband in his camp during the war.

WITNESS TO WAR

This is Sarah Osborn's account, a woman who played her part as a Patriot during the Siege of Yorktown. She stated that she:

" ... took her stand just back of the American tents, about a mile from the town, and busied herself with washing, mending, and cooking for the soldiers ..."

Do you think the work of washing, mending, and cooking was important during the time of war?

What impact may womens' contribution have had on the soldiers, both physically and mentally?

How do you think making such a contribution made women like Sarah feel?

CHAPTER 5

CHILDREN, FAMILIES, AND WAR

Life for children in the years before the American Revolution was hard. Children often had many chores and responsibilities at home. If their families owned or worked on farms, they were expected to help with tasks such as milking cows and gathering eggs.

Life Becomes Impossible

However, the American Revolution made life almost impossible for families who supported the king. They often had their property seized by Patriot groups. If they wanted to leave the colonies, they were not allowed to take their possessions with them. Even so, many fled to Canada. Yet, if they did leave, any sons over the age of 12 could be compelled to stay and fight for the Patriots.

Colonials lived mainly simple lives before the Revolution, but when war came close, homelife was uprooted and childhoods were changed overnight.

Some Patriot women fought to protect their homes. Anne Van Doren hit a drunk British officer on the head with a candlestick when he invaded her home!

It is said that another Patriot woman, Nancy Hart (shown below), took a rifle to the British soldiers who tried to take her home.

Changing Children's Lives

The American Revolution had a huge effect on the children who witnessed it. Many young men who would later fight for the Continental army had been children when the Sugar Act and Stamp Act were passed. Children saw their fathers and older brothers leave to fight, unsure if they would ever come back. They lived with constant fear and uncertainty.

The War Comes Home

When the American Revolution began, many men and teenage boys left to fight. This meant that the women and children left behind had to take on new roles and responsibilities. The Continental and British armies would fight wherever they met up, which was often near people's homes. Many families had to flee to safety with very little warning. Others were forced to let soldiers live in their homes.

Damaged and Destroyed

Not only did soldiers invade the homes of families, they also destroyed them. It is not known exactly how many homes and properties were damaged and destroyed during the war, but historians safely guess that the number reaches thousands.

A Childhood of War

Young people who grew up in the years of the American Revolution often had strong feelings about the war. Many teenage boys and young men signed up to fight as soon as the war began. Younger children, both boys and girls, found ways to support the war effort as well.

Battles and Boys

Starting at the age of 16, boys could join the Continental and British armies. Some volunteered to join. Others were **drafted**, or required to join, for a certain period of time. It was not unusual for boys under the age of 16 to make it onto the battlefield, though. Boys as young as nine years old could join the troops as drummer boys. Nathan Futrell was said to have been the youngest drummer boy during the war, joining the Continental army at just seven years old. Drummer boys were vital to both armies because the noise of their drumming could often be heard above the noise of the battle and traveled over long distances. The drumming was used as a form of code to carry messages that told troops what to do.

Drumming into Battle

Drums were an important way for soldiers to communicate on the battlefield. Certain drum patterns stood for certain commands. Drummer boys set the rhythm for marching and called soldiers to battle.

Drummer boys were in danger during battle, just like the soldiers, and many were killed.

Girl Fighters

Boys were not the only ones eager to support their side. Sybil Ludington's father was a militia commander. When Sybil was 16 years old, she rode 40 miles (64 km) through dangerous terrain in the middle of the night to gather her father's troops and warn them of a British attack. Though they were not allowed to join the army, other girls throughout the colonies supported soldiers however they could. They cooked for the troops and sewed their uniforms. They also acted as nurses for the wounded.

WITNESS TO WAR

Joseph Plumb Martin joined the Connecticut state militia at the age of 15 and the Continental army at 16. This is his account:

"The British took possession of a hill overlooking us ... During the night we remained in our trenches ... The water was nearly over my shoes by morning. Many of us took violent colds ... I had nothing to eat or drink, not even water. In the evening a messmate found me and brought me boiled hog's flesh and turnips."

Joseph came from a wealthy family. What effect do you think the difficult living conditions described in his account would have had on him?

Children had to help their mothers try and protect farms and livestock as battles raged nearby.

Beyond the Colonists

In the early stages of the American Revolution, most Native American tribes wanted to remain neutral—that is, they did not want to take sides in the conflict. Many soon realized, though, that an independent American country could be a bigger threat to their land and culture than the British colonies. Some Native American tribes decided to side with the colonists, but most favored the British because the British had promised to protect their lands from white settlers. During the war, many Native Americans were killed, either in battle, as retaliation by Patriot soldiers, or by starvation.

A Changed World

When the war was over, Native Americans did not get the protections they had hoped for. Instead, the United States continued to expand westward and many tribes were forced off their land. The policies of the newly created United States also forced Native American tribes to stop hunting and survive instead on agriculture, or growing crops. On July 13, 1775, the Second Continental Congress approved a speech to the Six Confederate Nations, a united group of Native American people. In it they ask Native Americans to stay neutral. The words of the speech are shown opposite.

> The struggle over land and freedom between the Patriots and British cost the Native American peoples dearly. It contributed to the further loss of their land and freedom.

"We desire you will hear and receive what we have now told you, and that you will open a good ear and listen to what we are now going to say. This is a family quarrel between us and Old England. You Indians are not concerned in it. We don't wish you to take up the hatchet against the king's troops. We desire you to remain at home, and not join on either side, but keep the hatchet buried deep."

PRIMARY SOURCE

Betrayal and Mistrust

This painting, created between 1771 and 1772, is called *The **Treaty** of Penn*. It depicts an agreement that was said to have been made between the Lenape Native American tribe and William Penn of Great Britain in 1682. The agreement was that the British and Lenape would live in peace forever. William Penn was a British colonist who founded the Province of Pennsylvania, and who believed in democracy and religious freedom. It is likely that if he did make the agreement, he intended to honor it. However, Penn's sons later destroyed the document, and **reneged** on the agreement. With such betrayals already experienced by the Native Americans, how do you think they may have felt about the speech to the Six Confederate Nations?

CHAPTER 6

BECOMING AMERICANS

After nearly eight years of fighting and many more of political unrest, the American Revolution ended in 1783. The British and the colonists signed a peace treaty and British troops left the former colonies. The new geographic boundaries of the country that would become the United States were set. For families that had once considered themselves British citizens, it was time to become Americans.

Turning Point at Yorktown

The last major battle was in September and October 1781. The British army, led by General Charles Cornwallis, had retreated to Yorktown, Virginia. The French, who were allies of the colonists, sent ships to Virginia to stop the British from leaving Yorktown. Meanwhile, George Washington marched his troops south toward Yorktown. The British were surrounded and outnumbered by the 18,000 Continental and French troops.

This reenactment is a reminder that although the colonists achieved their hard-won freedom, the cost of the victory was heavy, with great loss of life on both sides of the war.

WITNESS TO WAR

Dr James Thacher served in the Continental army and gave this account of the surrender of the British at Yorktown:

Mortification is another word for shame and embarrassment.

" ... the spirit and pride of the British soldier was put to the severest test: here their mortification could not be concealed ... many of the soldiers manifested a sullen temper, throwing their arms on the pile with violence, as if determined to render them useless ..."

Why do you think the British soldiers were so mortified at their defeat? What do you think they believed the outcome of the war would be and why?

On October 19, 1781, the British surrendered at Yorktown, and about 7,000 British troops were captured.

Signing for Peace

The British defeat at Yorktown convinced many in England that they should stop fighting. In February 1782, the British Parliament voted to end the war. In April, negotiations began between the British and the Americans. Benjamin Franklin, John Jay, Henry Laurens, and John Adams represented the Americans in the peace talks. After nearly a year and a half, on September 3, 1783, the Treaty of Paris was signed. The United States now included the land stretching down to Florida in the south, what is now Canada to the north, and the Mississippi River to the west.

Building America

During the American Revolution, the Continental Congress had written a framework for a new government called the Articles of Confederation. It was an agreement between the 13 states (former colonies), that dealt with issues such as taxes that would be paid, and how each state would vote to pass laws that applied to the entire country. It also said that all 13 states had to agree before the Articles of Confederation could be amended, or changed.

Making a New System

Once the United States had won the Revolution and began to fully function as a new country, the Articles of Confederation were found to have many problems. The Congress did not have the structure or powers to raise money by collecting taxes, or to force states to follow laws that were created.

The Constitution Is Born

In 1787, it was decided that a new framework was needed. A convention was called to create it. After months of debate and compromises, the **US Constitution** was written and approved by the convention delegates. It then went to the states for ratification. Nine states needed to ratify it before the Constitution was accepted. On June 21, 1788, the ninth state **ratified** it, and the Constitution took effect in 1789. By 1790, the thirteenth and last state, Rhode Island, ratified the document.

The original Constitution created the framework for the government of the United States.

This painting shows the signing of the Constitution by convention delegates in 1787.

Government Framework

The US Constitution is short compared to the constitutions of many other countries, at 4,400 words, but it lays the framework for how US government still works today. Most notably, it limits the power of government in favor of "the people." When it came into force in 1789 it replaced the Articles of Confederation (see page 38). In the Constitution, the federal, or central, government is divided into three branches— legislative, executive, and judicial.

How It Works

The legislative branch includes the Congress and makes the laws. The executive branch includes the president and enforces the laws. The judicial branch, which includes the Supreme Court, interprets the laws. By dividing the government into three branches, the Constitution ensures that no one person or group becomes too powerful. Power is also shared between the federal government and state governments. This helps deal with localized issues and accommodates diverse viewpoints across such a large country.

Shaping a New Country

The men who would become the first five presidents of the United States had all played a major part in the Revolution. The sixth, John Quincy Adams, was a child during the war, and watched the Battle of Bunker Hill from the top of a hill when he was just seven years old! The men, women, and children who lived through the American Revolution would go on to shape the government that we live with today.

Important Rights

Though the Constitution was eventually ratified by all 13 states, not everyone believed that it was perfect. Many were concerned that it did not protect certain freedoms. As a solution, ten **amendments** were added in 1791. These first 10 amendments are called the Bill of Rights. Many of the freedoms and protections that we now take for granted are listed in the Bill of Rights.

John Quincy Adams saw the birth of a new country and would spend the rest of his life serving it.

PRIMARY SOURCE

The Fight for Freedoms

One of the freedoms listed in the Bill of Rights (below) is the freedom of speech, which allows people to speak out against the government without the fear of being arrested. The people who demanded this freedom had lived through the Revolution, and the divisions and violence between those who supported the British and those who chose independence. Why do you think the freedom to speak out and express an opinion was so important to the people who had witnessed the American Revolution?

Congress of the United States,

WITNESS TO WAR

William Cooper was an American land merchant who bought and sold land near Albany, New York. He witnessed firsthand the hardship of settlers:

"In May, 1786, I opened the sales of forty thousand acres, which, in sixteen days, were all taken up by the poorest order of men. I ... went to live among them ... their maize did not ripen; their wheat was blasted, and the little they did gather they had no mill to grind within twenty miles distance; not one in twenty had a horse, and the way lay through rapid streams, across swamps, or over bogs."

Do you think their victory in the American Revolution would have encouraged settlers to persevere through such difficulties? Give reasons for your answer.

Life in America after the Revolution threw up many challenges, both for the settlers and Native Americans who already inhabited the land. This image from 1793 shows Native Americans traveling with settlers by canoe past settlements that had been established.

1775

LEXINGTON

More than 25,000 American soldiers lost their lives during the American Revolution on battlefields such as Lexington.

Lasting Legacy

The American Revolution is the war that created America. It shaped US laws, the way citizens vote in elections and choose representatives in government, and the freedoms that the United States protects. We live with its legacy and effects every day.

The Cost of War

Between 25,000 and 50,000 colonial soldiers were killed during the American Revolution. At least 8,000, though possibly many more, died on the battlefield. Another 17,000 were killed by disease or starvation. The casualties on the British side were about the same, with most deaths due to disease.

Brave Sacrifices

As with so many wars, the American Revolution was much more than a list of battles lost or won. It was an uneven struggle for independence, only achieved through the courage and sacrifices of those who fought in the Continental army and the militias, and the women and children who supported them and took on new roles and responsibilities.

Loss and Changes

Almost everyone who lived through and witnessed the American Revolution suffered great personal losses as each side fought for the cause they believed in. All had to cope with the changes and adjustments of fighting against a country they had once called their own.

Shining a Light

For all of the suffering and hardship that the war brought colonial families, much was also gained. Together, the citizens of the newly formed country worked to build a new country and unique system of government. For more than 200 years, the framework and government structure they created has both endured and influenced the governments of other countries. Their contributions are felt every day, around the world and here at home. And their accounts as witnesses to history shine a light on the past for us today.

Memorials to the people who lost their lives and statues commemorating great leaders of the American Revolution, such as George Washington, remember the cause and those who fought for it.

A TIMELINE FOR WAR

This timeline charts the key events of the American Revolution.

1754 — **May 28:** The French and Indian War begins in North America with the Battle of Jumonville Glen. Though Great Britain would win, it emerged from the conflict deep in debt.

1763 — **October 7:** George III issues a proclamation, designed to protect Native American land, which forbids the colonists from settling further west than the Appalachian Mountains.

1764 — **April 5:** The Sugar Act is passed by the British Parliament, enforcing taxes on imported sugar and increasing taxes on coffee and wine.

1765 — **March 22:** The British Parliament passes the Stamp Act—a direct tax on colonists, many of whom become concerned about "taxation without representation." It is repealed the next year.

1770 — **March 5:** Five colonists are shot and killed by British soldiers in the Boston Massacre.

1773 — **December 16:** A mob of colonists dump hundreds of crates of British tea into Boston Harbor in what will become known as the Boston Tea Party.

1774 — **September 5:** Delegates to the First Continental Congress meet in Philadelphia.

1775

April 18: The engraver Paul Revere rides to alert colonial forces to the advance of British troops.

April 19: The battles of Lexington and Concord are fought.

May 10: The Second Continental Congress assembles in Philadelphia.

June 15: George Washington is named commander-in-chief of the Continental army.

June 17: The Battle of Bunker Hill is fought—the British win but suffer heavy losses.

1776

January 10: Thomas Paine's pamphlet *Common Sense* is published. It sets out clearly why the colonies should become independent from Great Britain.

July 4: The Declaration of Independence is ratified by the Continental Congress.

August 27: In the Battle of Long Island, the British drive back the Americans.

December 26: Washington launches a surprise attack in Trenton, New Jersey, and gains an important American victory. Eight days later, he again defeats the British at Princeton.

1780

September 25: As the war continues, Continental army general Benedict Arnold's plans to surrender West Point to British forces are found out. He escapes and becomes a brigadier general in the British army.

1781

March 1: The Articles of Confederation are ratified by the Continental Congress. The document will later be replaced by the US Constitution.

1783

September 3: The Treaty of Paris is signed and ends the American Revolution.

GLOSSARY

alliance a group joining forces to work together

amendments additions or changes to a document, law, or set of laws, such as the Constitution

artillery cannons, large guns, or other weapons for firing over long distances

boycotts joining with others in refusing to buy from or deal with a person, nation, or business

casualties people who are injured or killed in an accident or war

charter an official document that sets out rights and establishes principles and rules

charter colonies colonies governed by an official document from the king, which sets out the rules

colonies areas of land controlled and often occupied by another—usually distant—country

committee a group of people directed to oversee or consider a matter

delegates representatives elected to attend a political gathering

draft a nonfinal version of an official document

drafted recruited and forced to fight

Loyalists people who were faithful to the British Crown during the American Revolution

militia a group of volunteer or citizen soldiers, organized to assemble in emergencies

Parliament in England, the group of politicians who establish the country's laws

Patriots American colonists who believed in independence— separating from British rule

proprietary colonies privately owned colonies or settlements

ratified officially approved

reneged went back on a promise or agreement

repealed withdrew and did away with (a law)

resources useful supplies of things that occur in nature, such as wood or animal furs

royal colonies colonies controlled by a British governor, appointed by the king

Sons of Liberty a secretive group of American colonists who organized widespread and sometimes violent protests against the British government's taxes and unfair treatment

taxes money added to the price of something or paid directly to fund government spending

treaty an official, signed agreement between two or more groups or countries

US Constitution a document adopted in 1789 that explains the different parts of the US government and how each part works

FIND OUT MORE

Books

Boutland, Craig. *The American Revolution* (America Goes to War). Rosen Publishing Group, 2023.

DK. *American Revolution* (DK Eyewitness). DK Children, 2022.

Murray, Katlin. *Was the American Revolution Revolutionary?* (Key Questions in American History). Rosen Publishing Group, 2019.

Websites

Find out more about the American Revolution at:
kids.britannica.com/kids/article/American-Revolution/353711

Learn about the people and events of the Revolution at:
www.dkfindout.com/us/history/american-revolution

Discover more about the Constitution of the United States at:
http://bensguide.gpo.gov/u-s-constitution-1789

Publisher's note to educators and parents:
All the websites featured above have been carefully reviewed to ensure that they are suitable for students. However, many websites change often, and we cannot guarantee that a site's future contents will continue to meet our high standards of educational value. Please be advised that students should be closely monitored whenever they access the Internet.

INDEX

About the Author

Kelly Roberts has written many history books for young people. In researching the eyewitness accounts in this book, she has learned more about the human experience of war and the devastation it caused for those who witnessed it.

SLIMY AND SMELLY

ANIMAL WEAPONS AND DEFENSES

by Mari Bolte

CAPSTONE PRESS
a capstone imprint

Published by Capstone Press, an imprint of Capstone
1710 Roe Crest Drive, North Mankato, Minnesota 56003
capstonepub.com

Library of Congress Cataloging-in-Publication Data
Names: Bolte, Mari, author.
Title: Slimy and smelly animal weapons and defenses / Mari Bolte.
Description: North Mankato : Capstone Press, 2024. | Series: Shockingly strange animal
weapons and defenses | Includes bibliographical references and index. | Audience:
Ages 9-11 | Audience: Grades 4-6 | Summary: "In a battle to survive, sometimes an
animal's best defense is to gross out the enemy. From poop and slime to puke and gas,
these slimy and smelly animal adaptations allow some disgusting animals to live to fight
another day"— Provided by publisher.
Identifiers: LCCN 2023054394 (print) | LCCN 2023054395 (ebook) | ISBN 9781669078326
(hardcover) | ISBN 9781669078272 (paperback) | ISBN 9781669078289 (pdf) | ISBN
9781669078302 (kindle edition) | ISBN 9781669078296 (epub)
Subjects: LCSH: Animal defenses—Juvenile literature. | Predatory animals—Effect of
odors on—Juvenile literature.
Classification: LCC QL759 .B64 2024 (print) | LCC QL759 (ebook) | DDC 591.47—dc23/
eng/20231128
LC record available at https://lccn.loc.gov/2023054394
LC ebook record available at https://lccn.loc.gov/2023054395

Editorial Credits
Editor: Mandy Robbins; Designer: Dina Her; Media Researcher: Jo Miller;
Production Specialist: Tori Abraham

Image Credits
Alamy: All Canada Photos, 27, Avalon.red, 29, Bill Gorum, 18, blickwinkel, 21, Nature
Picture Library, 17, 23, Piotr Krzeslak, 15; Getty Images: Henrik_L, 12; Nature Picture
Library: Morley Read, 22, Tony Wu, 5; Science Source: Tom McHugh, 24; Shutterstock:
Dmitry Fch, 8, Doikanoy, 10, FoxGrafy, design element (throughout), Jay Ondreicka,
Cover, (bottom), johannviloria, Cover, (top left), Martin Pelanek, Cover, (top right),
mumunha, 9, Ryan M. Bolton, 26, Vojce, 20, Wirestock Creators, 7, Wulan Rohmawati, 11

Printed and bound in China. 5827

TABLE OF CONTENTS

Words in **bold** are in the glossary.

DISGUSTING DEFENSES

Imagine being chased. You want to get away. You could run. Or you could gross out your attacker!

SPERM WHALES

Sperm whales make a poo-nado. They poop and then spin in circles. The poop cloud can stretch more than 100 feet (30.5 meters) across. Grossing out the enemy gives the whale time to swim away.

POOP POWER

SKIPPER CATERPILLARS

Skipper caterpillars are only 2 inches (5 centimeters) long at most. But they can shoot poop more than 40 times that length! A **hatch** on their backside opens and closes. Little nuggets of poop shoot out.

BURROWING OWL

Some animals use poop to attract **prey**. Burrowing owls eat dung beetles. Dung beetles eat poop. The owls collect the poop of other animals. Dung beetles follow their noses. The beetles don't realize they are the meal until it is too late.

ASIAN HONEYBEE

Asian honeybees work hard to build their nests. But a big **predator** can take down a beehive in just hours.

The bees put poop around the hive openings. This makes the hive less appealing to enemies like hornets.

TORTOISE BEETLE LARVA

Tortoise beetle **larva** are fighters. They use their skin and poop in battle!

As they grow, they shed their skins. But they don't throw them away! The larva use their poop to glue old skin to their bodies. They swing the poop shield at predators.

SOMETHING SMELLS

HOOPOE

Hoopoe birds are stunning but smelly! Females have a **gland** that makes a waxy brown goo. The goo smells like rotten meat.

The bird coats her feathers in goo. It makes them waterproof. She covers her eggs in it too. The goo protects the chicks inside from **bacteria**.

LESSER ANTEATER

Predators stay away when they smell an anteater. Like skunks, anteaters spray when in danger. But a lesser anteater is four to seven times smellier! That's not their only stink, though. Anteater poop is extra nasty.

FUN FACT

Lesser anteaters are also known as the "stinkers of the forest."

WESTERN HOOK-NOSED SNAKE

Some snakes hiss or rattle to warn predators away. The western hook-nosed snake's best defense is a fart!

The snake's fart sounds like a human's, but it's higher-pitched. The release of air can help the snake move its body quickly.

SUPER SLIMY

SEA HARE

Danger approaches. The sea hare's weak eyes can only see light or dark. It doesn't worry, though. Its body is covered in **toxic** slime. An animal that touches it could become very sick or even die.

FUN FACT

The sea hare also shoots out a cloud of dark purple goo. This gives it time to get away from predators.

VELVET WORMS

Velvet worms are full of goo. They shoot the sticky slime at prey. The worm swings itself back and forth like a sprinkler. The slime hardens within seconds. Any prey caught in the slime is instantly trapped.

HAGFISH

Hagfish look like easy meals. But they don't go down without a fight! They can make a bucket's worth of slime in an instant. The slime is made from threads. The threads expand to 10,000 times their original size. The slime makes the hagfish super slippery.

FUN FACT

Hagfish slime is deadly. Fish can choke on it. But hagfish can die if they get trapped in it too.

ACID WASH

VINEGAROONS

Vinegaroons got their name from the vinegar-like **acid** in their bodies. These insects spray the acid at predators. It can cause rashes and short-term blindness. That's usually enough to take vinegaroons off an animal's menu.

BOMBARDIER BEETLES

Bombardier beetles have different **chemicals** inside their bodies. If attacked, the beetle shoots them out its backside. Together, the chemicals make a boiling acid. The beetle can send up to 500 bursts a second!

The acid can kill insects and scare enemies. Toads that eat the beetles barf them back up.

FUN FACT

The chemicals are kept separate inside the beetle. If they mix too soon, they kill the beetle.

GLOSSARY

acid (A-suhd)—a strong liquid that can break down tissue

bacteria (bak-TEER-ee-uh)—very small living things that exist everywhere in nature; some are helpful, and some are harmful

chemical (KE-muh-kuhl)—relating to the basic substances that make up all materials

gland (GLAND)—an organ in the body that makes certain chemicals

hatch (HACH)—an opening that can open and close

larva (LAR-vuh)—an insect at the stage of development between an egg and an adult

predator (PRED-uh-tur)—an animal that hunts other animals for food

prey (PRAY)—an animal hunted by another animal for food

toxic (TOK-sik)—poisonous

READ MORE

MacCarald, Clara. *Getting Smelly to Survive*. Minneapolis: Kids Core, an imprint of Abdo Publishing, 2023.

Shragg, Karen. *Nature's Yucky! In the Sea: Gross Stuff that Helps Ocean Animals Survive*. Missoula, MT: Mountain Press Publishing Company, 2023.

Silver, Erin. *Mighty Scared: The Amazing Ways Animals Defend Themselves*. Custer, WA: Orca Book Publishers, 2024.

INTERNET SITES

10 Weirdest Animal Defense Mechanisms
youtube.com/watch?v=p9y0QKz4d3Y

Extreme Animal Weapons
pbs.org/wgbh/nova/video/extreme-animal-weapons/

San Diego Wildlife Alliance: Ooh That Smell
stories.sandiegozoo.org/zoonooz/ooh-that-smell/

INDEX

ABOUT THE AUTHOR

Mari Bolte is the author and editor of hundreds of children's books. Every book is her favorite book as long as the readers learned something and enjoyed themselves!